Wheels Around Arran, Bute and Cu

by
Robert Grieves

A mid-1970s scene taken in Balloch Crescent, Millport, near the junction with Provost's Loan, which at that time was a new housing development. The pavement and the street are being surfaced, the materials for which were delivered by Cumbrae Transport which served the Millport area during that decade. GSJ 327N was a 1975 Leyland Clydesdale in the blue livery of this associate company of Arran Transport, which operated both road haulage and passenger transport on that island. Just visible to the right is an Aveling–Barford mechanical roller, hired from McCarrol of Bishopbriggs who have long specialised in this type of work. (Walter Kerr.)

© Robert Grieves 2004
First published in the United Kingdom, 2004,
by Stenlake Publishing Ltd.
Telephone: 01290 551122
Printed by Cordfall Ltd., Glasgow, G21 2QA

ISBN 1 84033 326 X

A bird's-eye view of Rothesay's Guildford Square in 1903, only a year after electric trams were introduced to replace the original horse-drawn cars. At the town terminus is No. 19, one of the newly delivered crossbench style Brush cars. It awaits departure time before leaving for Port Bannatyne, while a similar tram approaches past the Winter Gardens and the Temperance Hotel. Also prominent in this view, waiting at the coach stance adjacent to the Ewing Fountain, is a four-in-hand open charabanc owned by McKirdy & McMillan and about to set out for Mount Stuart or Kilchattan Bay.

Front cover: Unmistakably Arran. With the island's highest mountain, Goatfell, as a backdrop, OB type Bedford SJ 1340 climbs the heather-clad hill from Brodick in the late afternoon of a sunny September day in 1965. The main road to Lamlash at that time had not been widened, but certainly carried much less traffic than today. When photographed, the Duple Vista-bodied 29 seater was owned by Lennox of Whiting Bay, but had previously been operated by Gordon Bros. of Lamlash from 1950 (when it was new) until 1961, at which stage the firm sold out to Lennox Motors. In 1967, Lennox in turn sold out to Arran Transport of Brodick and SJ 1340 continued in service there until withdrawn in 1970. Happily, this coach still exists, in the Scottish Vintage Bus Museum at Lathalmond near Dunfermline, where it is currently undergoing restoration by preservationists.

Inside front cover: A line of coaches hopefully awaits custom for island tours on a wet Rothesay day in August 1965. They were representative of the single-deck fleet of Western SMT on Bute at that period, and were based at Pointhouse garage in Ardbeg which had originally been the Rothesay Tramways depot. These vehicles (new in 1957) were unusual because the combination of their Bristol chassis and Alexander bodies was unique to Western.

FOREWORD

Wheels Around Arran, Bute and Cumbrae is sixteenth in this series and contains the usual mixture of nostalgic scenes of yesterday's transport. Grateful thanks are due to all the many mainly retired transport owners and employees who provided information to assist in its compilation.

Collectively, these islands in the Firth of Clyde comprised the former County of Bute, which ceased to exist after local government reorganisation in 1975. The motor vehicle license letters SJ were allocated to Buteshire in 1903 when the system was introduced. In 1963, the final year before suffix letters were in use, the numbers had only reached 2860, understandable in an area with a relatively small population. SJ 1 was issued in December 1903 to Andrew Graham Murray of Rothesay Terrace, Edinburgh, for his 8 h.p. De Dion phaeton, and was transferred to a Berliet car in January 1905 for the same owner (who became the Rt. Hon. Lord Dunedin). Numbers SJ 2–11 were allocated to a variety of owners either elsewhere in Scotland or in England. In July 1904 the first local number issued to someone who actually lived in the County of Bute was SJ 12, which belonged to an Ariel 15 h.p. wagonette owned by Lady Margaret Crichton-Stuart of Mount Stuart. On the Isle of Arran the first locally registered vehicle was SJ 34, a chain-driven Singer 3 h.p. motorcycle purchased by Robert Jamieson of Glencloy House, Brodick, in October 1905. The first car with a local number was SJ 108, a 12 h.p. Argyll phaeton built in Alexandria with Roi des Belges bodywork and bought by Robert Morrison of Miramar, Lamlash, in February 1911. Cumbrae's first SJ license was not issued until as late as May 1919 when SJ 206, a Radco 2¼ h.p. motorcycle, was bought by Dr James Herbert Paul of Kersland, Millport. Dr Paul also acquired the first locally registered car on Cumbrae – SJ 314 – in August 1921. As an aside, it is interesting to record that Bute is the only Scottish county apart from Orkney never to have introduced traffic lights, remaining without them to this day.

Jack Shearer of Crichton Street, Millport, operated tours around the Isle of Cumbrae, initially with horse-drawn landaus which were housed in the Miller Street stables. In the early 1920s he joined the motor age and purchased this 1-ton Ford charabanc which he named 'Thistle'. Jack is seen here in Cardiff Street opposite the pierhead awaiting the arrival of passengers and touting for custom for his 'Round the Island' tour. An advertising board in the nearside window of the chara prices the tour at 1s. 6d., as does the board propped up against the radiator. Another operator of landaus in Millport prior to the First World War was James Bartholomew of Eastwood. These vehicles were often used as taxis to and from the steamers before cars were introduced on the island, and as recently as the 1960s Mr MacGillivray of the former MacGillivray Arms Hotel in Stuart Street continued to operate one.

Paddle wheels approaching Arran in Edwardian days. Seen from the Brodick shore adjacent to the mouth of the Strathwhillan Burn is the Victorian paddle steamer *Glen Sannox* of 1892, which was built by J. & G. Thomson of Clydebank for the Glasgow & South Western Railway fleet. In the years of intense rivalry between the ferry companies, the *Sannox* vied with the Caledonian Railway's *Duchess of Hamilton* for passenger trade on the service from Ardrossan to Arran. Whereas the *Duchess* used Montgomerie Pier on the mainland, the *Sannox* sailed from Winton Pier, which is still today's departure point for the Arran crossing operated by Caledonian MacBrayne.

This 1903 scene at Shedog, Shiskine, typifies transport in the period prior to the advent of the motor vehicle on the Isle of Arran. Colin Currie's horse-drawn brake has just arrived after its journey from Brodick over the String Road, which involved a long climb and equally arduous descent across the centre of the island. Currie was the first operator on Arran to replace his horses with a motor charabanc, which was a new Albion purchased in 1913 and was the first such vehicle on the island, preceding the Jamieson Brothers' Commer (facing page) by a short head. Colin Currie – and later his son John – also operated several model T Ford cars (including SJ 186, 237, 347 and 402) as 'buses' on the service to Brodick in opposition to Bannatyne of Blackwaterfoot during the 1920s. These were superseded by larger Buick cars.

Kildonan, the southernmost village on Arran, was home to J. & J. Jamieson, proprietors of the Kildonan Hotel and owners of the island's second charabanc. This was the first locally licensed motor charabanc on Arran and was registered SJ 146. It was a 2-ton 20 h.p. Commer which arrived in June 1914, and must have been a colourful sight on the island's roads as it was finished in a lavender livery with the wheels painted in a straw shade. As with many of the other early motor vehicle operators, the Jamieson brothers had started in the horse era, operating a conveyance to and from the Kildonan Hotel. Their deaths in 1917 prompted the sale of SJ 146 to Hamilton of High Kildonan, making it the latter's first motor charabanc, which he used on his service between Lagg and Whiting Bay.

Caught by the camera on tour at the Corrie Hotel around 1920 is GA 1788, owned by Colin Currie of Shiskine. This was a solid-tyred chain-driven Albion charabanc, the second such vehicle to be owned by Currie. The driver is John Robertson, who had been the first man to drive a bus on Arran when Col Currie bought his original Albion in 1913.

A classic Edwardian scene showing a horse-drawn trap – or buggy as they were known on Arran – followed by a wagonette and a cart on the opening day of the new road bridge across the mouth of the Allt Gobhlach Burn, which flows into Kilbrannan Sound at Pirnmill. Robert Anderson may be seen at the reins of the buggy with his wife alongside. Robert was the local blacksmith and also owned the village store, which is just visible on the right of this view. His smiddy is the building to the left of the shop, seen in the process of conversion to the Anvil Tea Room (now known as the Lighthouse) by his son John. This photograph was by John Anderson, who took scenic views of the Pirnmill area and interesting vignettes of village life which today form an important record of social history. Many of these scenes were printed as picture postcards which were sold in the family shop.

Research through the early motor tax records for the County of Bute reveals that Fords were undoubtedly the most popular choice of vehicle on Arran, Bute and Cumbrae during the period prior to 1930. The main Ford agent and distributor for the area from 1920 to 1925 was to be found in what may appear to be a strange location, the small village of Pirnmill on the north-west coast of Arran. This was Robert Anderson, who operated a road passenger service to Lochranza in the 1920s in connection with the steamers, later continued by his son John. The photograph shows Anderson's Pirnmill premises, which combined the Ford agency and workshop and were located to the rear of their smiddy (facing page). The three employees are believed to be Duncan Kerr, Jim Walker and Charlie Robertson. Two model Ts are visible through the entrance and a solid-tyred Fordson tractor can be seen behind the glass-panelled door to the left. An advertising board outside the garage prices the tractor at £205. The model T was particularly popular on Arran and was often used as a 4-seat hackney car, while the larger model TT was pressed into service as a 14-seat charabanc or wagonette by many of the small public transport businesses which flourished on the island. This was especially true before the Road Traffic Act of 1930, which introduced much tighter licensing laws. Amongst the operators in the 1920s who owned Fords supplied by Anderson's were Currie, Shiskine; Weir, Machrie; Stewart, Corriecravie; Lennox, Whiting Bay; Ribbeck, Brodick; McBride, Pirnmill; McMillan, Pirnmill; Bannatyne, Blackwaterfoot; Hamilton, Kildonan; Currie, Lagg; and of course Robert Anderson himself.

A scene from around 1930 showing Brodick Bay with Arran's famous peak Goatfell rising behind. Activity at the old quay adjacent to the Strathwhillan Burn is caused by the arrival of the sailing smack *Betsy Crawford* with a cargo of coal from Irvine to be unloaded and distributed locally by means of the horse-drawn cart and two motor lorries (often a return cargo, frequently of potatoes, was shipped back from Arran). The lorries were a Ford and a Morris Commercial, believed to have been owned by carrier and contractor William Currie, while *Betsy Crawford* belonged to Captain Crawford of Corrie. At the time she was one of a fast-disappearing fleet of this type of coastal trading vessel, largely replaced by steam 'puffers', the famous little general cargo carriers so popular on Scotland's west coast as they could be readily beached at places without piers if necessary to load or unload. Neil Munro's *Vital Spark*, with her redoubtable skipper 'Para Handy', is of course the puffer everyone remembers.

SJ 1042 bustles from Brodick Pier en route to Pirnmill in summer 1953. At that time this 1946 Bedford OB was the regular performer on Weir's service across the String Road to Machrie and Pirnmill. This style of service bus bodywork was designed and constructed by Duple Motor Bodies of Hendon, but was also built by Arthur Mulliner of Northampton, better known perhaps as a coachbuilder of quality limousines. The lorry is VS 4731, a 1947 Austin two-tonner owned by local contractor Andrew McKelvie of Brodick. Austin taxis are visible on the cab rank, while the steamer in the background is the *Marchioness of Graham*.

The arrival of MV *Marchioness of Graham* from Ardrossan signals activity on Brodick Pier in 1953. In the foreground is BYS 36, owned by Weir of Machrie. This was a Duple-bodied Bedford WTB model of 1938 which had previously worked in the fleet of Fitzpatrick, Dunoon. Also visible is Weir's SJ 1042 (seen on the previous page) and the rear of a Duple-bodied Bedford OB type belonging to Lennox of Whiting Bay. In 1957 major changes came to Brodick with the inauguration of the first 'proper' car ferry, MV *Glen Sannox*, improving services to and from the mainland and benefiting the whole island.

Until the advent of the MV *Glen Sannox*, the first purpose-built car ferry to serve Arran, this is how motor vehicles were transported to and from the island. This late 1930s scene shows HS 8664, a 1935 Hillman at the aft end of the promenade deck of the previous TS *Glen Sannox* of 1925 as she departs Brodick Pier. Traffic was driven on and off the vessel over strategically placed planks between ship and shore, which was occasionally a hazardous business.

Bedfords at Brodick, 1953. Having loaded up at the pierhead after the arrival of the steamer, an assortment of colourful buses gets set to depart for various villages on Arran. Closest to the camera is SJ 1288, a 1949 OB model with Mulliner bodywork in the dark blue livery with red band and light blue roof of Gordon Brothers, Lamlash, whose destination is Whiting Bay. Next is SJ 895, in the light blue colours of Ernest Ribbeck of Brodick. This was a 1937 Duple-bodied WTB model on the Lochranza service, and is seen alongside red and cream SJ 1042 of Weir Bros., Machrie, which was a Duple bus-bodied OB type of 1946 which served Pirnmill. Furthest away is SJ 864, a 1936 WT type 3-ton lorry, also a member of Ribbeck's fleet. Just beyond the lorry a notice at the pier entrance which reads 'Pier dues 3*d*.' may be seen. Today, the most important crossing to the mainland is that between Brodick and Ardrossan and accordingly virtually all of the island's bus traffic centres on Brodick. Formerly, however, when passenger vessels called at several Arran villages, the pattern was very different, explaining the variety of locations of bus operators on the island, particularly in the pre-war decades. **11**

Puddles on the pier and raincoats suggest a wet Brodick day in summer 1953. The Pier Garage had been owned by Neil McBride of Brodick (who operated a Lochranza service) until 1930, when it was sold to Finlay Kerr-Newton. It passed to Lennox of Whiting Bay in 1951 and then to Arran Transport in the 1960s, in whose hands it remains today as a car-hire facility. Here passengers walk to join an incoming steamer, while the two buses await custom on its arrival. On the left is FGD 203 of Bannatyne Motors, a 1947 Bedford OB previously in the fleet of Northern Roadways of Glasgow which had bodywork built by SMT of Edinburgh to Duple design. It worked the Blackwaterfoot service, acquired in 1952 from Ribbeck's of Brodick, whose SJ 962 will depart for Lochranza once the boat arrives. This was a late example of the Bedford WTB model, but fitted with the new-style radiator of the OB type which was introduced shortly before the war in 1939. Bodywork by Duple of Hendon featured 'quarter lights' on either side of the roof, and Ribbeck's trademark 'bluebird' motif is visible too. Ribbeck's bus services and vehicles were sold to Arran Transport in 1966, while Bannatyne Motors was the last of the island operators to sell out, succumbing to Arran Transport in 1973. The bus scene on Arran today is covered by Stagecoach, who have been the sole provider of services since 1994.

These adverts are for two of the many public transport operators which served the Isle of Arran in the days when rivalry was quite intense and steamers calling at the various island piers were met by a number of bus owners whose colourful vehicles each carried their own distinctive liveries. One of the best-known names amongst Arran's busmen was Ernest Ribbeck of Brodick, who had started a horse-drawn mail and passenger service to Corrie as far back as the 1870s, progressing to motor transport early in the twentieth century. This advert shows SJ 895, a Duple-bodied Bedford WTB bought in 1937 and primarily used for 'Round Arran' tours for over twenty years. Ribbeck's post-war livery was blue and cream with a bluebird motif.

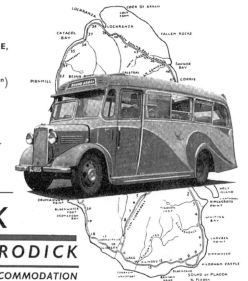

Initially operating in opposition to Ribbeck, but later in conjunction with him on the Brodick–Lochranza service, was Finlay Kerr-Newton, who shared this route from the 1930s until the early 1950s under the 'North Arran Motors' banner when he sold to Lennox of Whiting Bay. Lennox took over the Brodick Pier Garage and several of Newton's fleet including this pre-war Duple-bodied Bedford WTB.

Alexander Craig Lennox of Whiting Bay operated a predominantly Bedford fleet but also owned SJ 1212, a Commer Commando 30-seat coach of 1948, bodied by Strachan of Acton, north London. It is seen climbing to Lennox's garage, with Whiting Bay Pier in the background where a puffer is unloading its cargo. This was the final pier built on Arran (in 1899) and was the longest in the Firth of Clyde, allowing it to accommodate vessels when the tide was low. Steamer traffic here was never as busy as at Brodick and the last vessel called in 1962, with the pier being closed and demolished shortly afterwards. Lennox's had a long tradition of public service on Arran, having operated between Brodick and Whiting Bay from the early 1920s until selling out to Arran Transport in 1967. The firm also provided 'Round Arran' tours, as did several other operators on the island. These 56-mile circular excursions always proceeded anticlockwise, thus reducing the danger of buses having to pass at awkward places on the narrow roads. Although the days of a 7' 6" width limit are over, many sections of the island's roads are no wider today than when motorbuses first arrived in Arran, and yet must cope with vehicles of much larger dimensions than ever before.

Approaching Blackwaterfoot from Lochranza in 1953 along the shore of Kilbrannan Sound is SJ 1190, a Commer Commando with one of the very few examples on the island of bodywork by Harrington of Hove. This bus was operated by Peter McMillan of Woodside, Pirnmill, but had been new in 1948 to Donald Robertson of Harbour View, Blackwaterfoot, and continued to carry his ivory and black colours. McMillan had previously been a driver for Robertson's Bus Service and took over the Lochranza route after the death of his former employer in the early 1950s. Coincidentally, back in 1930, Robertson had acquired both the run operated by Peter McMillan's father, Jimmy, between Pirnmill and Lochranza in opposition to John Anderson (see page 7), and also Anderson's Imachar to Lochranza service. Robertson had used a Commer, a couple of Thornycrofts and a Bean amongst his earlier fleet. Peter McMillan's service passed to Weir of Machrie in the late 1950s, but his Commer buses were acquired by Ernest Ribbeck.

Seven buses are visible in this photograph taken at Lochranza pierhead in June 1966, lined up awaiting the arrival of passengers from the *Duchess of Hamilton*. Facing the camera on the left is blue-liveried SJ 1298, a 1949 Plaxton-bodied Commer Avenger belonging to Ernest Ribbeck of Brodick, with his 1948 Duple-bodied Albion, CHH 740, just visible behind. Next on the left is Lennox's SJ 1340, the 1950 Bedford OB/Duple seen on the front cover, then JVA 890, a Duple-bodied Albion Victor also owned by Lennox which had been new to Hutchison of Overtown in 1954. On the right are three SB type Bedfords, all bodied by Duple, and all in Lennox's maroon-liveried fleet, headed by PTN 662 of 1952. Alex C. Lennox had given up farming in Lanarkshire around 1903 to settle in Whiting Bay, where he started general contracting work with a horse and cart then steadily built up the business to include hiring ponies and traps, horses and wagonettes and a coach and pair. As the motor age progressed, Lennox bought a new Albion charabanc in 1919, and in 1923 the firm built the Pier Garage at Whiting Bay. Over the years Lennox's grew to become the largest bus operator on the island, but eventually Lennox Transport sold out to Haddow's growing Arran Transport Company in 1967. Lochranza ceased to be such an important focal point for buses in the north of Arran after regular steamer sailings stopped calling at the close of the 1971 summer season. Although a ferry across the Kilbrannan Sound to Claonaig in Kintyre started in July 1972 it generated very little traffic for Arran Transport, which by the following year was the only bus operator on the island.

Charles Weir of Machrie was another well-known name in transport circles on the Isle of Arran. Early motor vehicles in his fleet included two model T Ford 14-seat buses, one of which was bodied by James Martin of Kirkintilloch and operated the Machrie–Brodick service. This photograph shows Weir's Scottish Aviation-bodied Commer, GUS 129 of 1949, on a stormy September afternoon in 1965 when I travelled in it from Lochranza. As I was the sole passenger apart from one other, we were transferred at Weir's Machrie garage (where this view was taken) into NAJ 640, their 1955 Vauxhall Wyvern car for the remainder of the journey across the String Road to Brodick to connect with the evening ferry for Ardrossan. In 1966 Weir's red buses disappeared when the family sold its passenger transport operations to Bannatyne of Blackwaterfoot.

The name Bannatyne has for long been synonymous with transport and travel on the Isle of Arran. John Sillars Bannatyne of the Temperance Hotel, Blackwaterfoot, started his bus service in 1923 with SJ 401, a red 15-seater Fiat with an open charabanc style body and a hood (very important in Arran weather). Next came a second-hand Reo Speed Wagon with a similar style of body. Both were painted in a maroon shade. Former driver the late Archie McGillivray told of how he would often make four trips a day back and forward over 'the String' connecting with the steamers at Brodick, the service calling via Torbeg if required, then via Shiskine. If Dan Bannatyne was on board, it was not unknown for him to ask the driver to stop at Glenloig, about halfway on the journey, so he could collect one of the sheep he grazed there, and if the other passengers got too restless then they would be delivered to their destination and Archie would return for Dan and the sheep. All very informal and certainly not liable to occur today. J. S. Bannatyne sold the business in the mid-1930s, but in the early 1950s another generation of Bannatynes took over Ribbeck's Blackwaterfoot garage and the bus service to Brodick. The picture below shows GVA 635, one of three similar Albion Victor buses with Scottish Aviation bodywork which operated D. S. & D. E. Bannatyne's services in the 1960s and 70s in their green, red and cream colours (which were also applied to the lorry fleet). It is seen here just outside Blackwaterfoot, dropping off a schoolboy from Arran High School. (A. J. Douglas)

From 1953 the Bannatynes also operated a small fleet of lorries for the transport of milk from Arran farms to Torrylinn creamery at Kilmory. In the upper view, Donald S. Bannatyne is pictured outside Blackwaterfoot Garage with ASD 653, the second-hand 1944 Bedford O-type which started the milk runs. It is well-laden with ten-gallon milk cans, or churns as they were sometimes known, which were usually made ready for collection on a stand at their road-end by the farmers. Across the road is John S. Bannatyne's hotel (now the Blackwaterfoot Lodge), while the building to the left was the garage which had housed his buses in the 1920s and 30s. This is now a private house, the Old Stables. Bannatyne's still carry the island's milk to the creamery, as Donald Bannatyne Jnr. is now the owner of Arran Haulage Services Ltd. which operates milk tankers in addition to a lorry fleet. 'DS' recalls that in the 1950s there were over eighty dairy farms on the island, whereas today there are only four.

Heading home to Corriecravie from Lamlash (despite the unchanged destination) is SJ 749, sporting the blue and cream colours of Donald Stewart, Corriecravie. This was a Commer Centaur 20-seater with bodywork by John Stewart of Wishaw which had been new in 1933 and was in its twentieth year of service on Arran when photographed with driver Ian MacKenzie near the Ashdale Bridge, Whiting Bay. Seen in the background is the village's long pier, which was still a port of call for Clyde steamers until 1962, while across the bay rises the bulk of the Holy Isle.

Donald Stewart of Corriecravie was the southernmost operator on the Isle of Arran, providing services between Lamlash and Blackwaterfoot via the south Arran villages. Stewart had started business in 1902 running horse brakes between Corriecravie and Lamlash via the Ross Road from Sliddery through Glen Scorrodale. The photograph shows SJ 1081, a 1946 Bedford OB with Duple Vista-style bodywork, but built by SMT of Edinburgh and finished in the blue and cream (with green band) livery of Stewart's Motors, and seen at their premises in the small village of Corriecravie. Just visible beyond in the gloom of the garage is XS 5517, a Paisley-registered wartime Bedford OY type lorry of 1943 which also belonged to Stewart, as did the Austin hackney car outside. The coach and its twin (SJ 1082) passed to Bannatyne of Blackwaterfoot when that firm acquired Stewart's business in 1960.

A Stewart's Motors advertisement from around 1950.

In 1861 Andrew McKirdy founded what was to become the most important carriage hiring business in Rothesay. This was originally located on the site of today's bandstand but moved to Bishop Street in 1872. Andrew was succeeded by his son Hugh in 1888, by which time a large stud of saddle and carriage horses had been built up. Hugh continued to expand the business with a growing fleet of landaus, phaetons, wagonettes and four-in-hand brakes. In 1898 he joined forces with James McMillan, an Irishman from Ballymoney in Co. Antrim who had settled in Bute at Kilchattan Bay, where he started stables and a similar carriage hiring business. The partnership only lasted a relatively short time but the joint name of McKirdy & McMillan continued for goodwill purposes and is still in use today, over a century later. The company's large number of horses were stabled in premises at Kilchattan Bay and at Rothesay in the High Street where the police station now stands, as well as on the site of the former Ritz cinema. McKirdy & McMillan's current address in East Princes Street was also a stables, the site of which may still be seen to the rear of the premises. The Kilchattan stables later housed charabancs when M&M joined the motor age, and later still became a sub-depot for Western SMT buses where the last arrival and first departure for Rothesay was garaged (latterly a double-decker). A bungalow now covers the site. This Edwardian scene shows a typical horse-drawn bench-seated charabanc owned by McKirdy & McMillan heading back to town along Mount Stuart Road with a good complement of well-dressed passengers.

The hamlet of Kerrycroy with its village green and half-timbered Tudor-style houses was modelled on a typical English village by the wife of the second Marquess of Bute. Seen in early Edwardian times at the entrance to the village is one of McKirdy & McMillan's horse-drawn wagonettes. It faces the direction of Rothesay, no doubt returning there after an excursion to Mount Stuart. The passengers, as may be seen, were perched high above the wheels which allowed them to enjoy a commanding view of the passing countryside. The bench seating was reached by means of a portable ladder moved as necessary by the conductor. When this postcard was sent in 1907 the number of horses owned by M&M totalled 75. Their annual trading report of that year revealed that the 'carriage department' comprised 28 horses, 22 landaus, 1 Victoria, 1 brougham, 5 wagonettes, 2 hearses, 1 mourning coach, 5 polo carts and 7 vans. Their 'omnibus department' operated 47 horses, 24 charabancs and 6 closed omnibuses. During the winter season of 1909/10 the company operated a former London double deck horse bus, with back to back 'knifeboard' style seating on the upper deck, reached by a spiral staircase which was a 'test of one's sobriety' according to the reminiscences of a late former resident of Craigmore. He also recalled that amusingly it still displayed its former London destination boards.

Apart from a very short-lived example that appeared in 1898, the first motorbus on the Isle of Bute was delivered to McKirdy & McMillan in April 1909. Painted green, SJ 30 was a solid-tyred Halley built in Yoker with an open toastrack style body similar to the Rothesay tramcars. This registration had originally been allocated to a motorcycle in 1905, but when cancelled was reissued to the bus, which was common practice at the time with Bute and some other local authorities. The vehicle proved an immediate success and was followed by two more Halleys and a variety of other charabancs including a Commer, Daimlers and Albions. Initially of course the buses shared duties with the existing fleet of traditional horse-drawn transport. For instance in 1910 a half-hourly frequency was advertised to Kilchattan Bay jointly operated by motor and horse charabancs. As the

proportion of motorbuses gradually increased, so the number of horse vehicles decreased – a trend which escalated in the 1920s as the proportion of motors mushroomed. McKirdy & McMillan's final remaining horses were sold in the 1930s and Duncan Cameron, who was the last of the coachmen, went on to drive the company's motorbuses. Prominent in the centre of this photograph is James McMillan, proprietor of the company, who also served as provost of Rothesay between 1915 and 1921. This was the Halley's inaugural run to Mount Stuart, and accordingly it was fully laden with local businessmen and surrounded by a crowd of interested spectators eager to witness the occasion. The earlier motor service mentioned above was operated briefly in the summer season of 1898 by the grandly named Glasgow & West of Scotland Motor Car Co. Ltd. using two eight-seat Daimler wagonettes assembled and bodied in the Hamilton coachworks of John Stirling. They ran between Rothesay and Mount Stuart but apparently broke down regularly, and the venture soon ended with the vehicles returning to the mainland. Horses reigned supreme for a further decade.

V 6643 was one of McKirdy & McMillan's pre-First World War solid-tyred Albion charabancs, seen at Kerrycroy shore in the early 1920s with driver Neil Paton and a short-trousered schoolboy conductor whose identity is not known. When the island was at its busiest with visitors during the summer school holiday period it was quite common for local boys to be employed as conductors. To collect the fares they had to make their way precariously along the running boards of the charabancs, as these vehicles had no centre passageways. Naturally enough this provided added excitement to a job which the boys generally enjoyed. Accessories such as a cash bag over their shoulder and sometimes even a peaked cap helped to give them an additional grown-up feeling. Before the pier at Rothesay was built, an important ferry link to the mainland was between Kerrycroy and Largs.

Ettrick Bay on the west coast of Bute was reached by Rothesay's red electric trams in July 1905 when the extended line from the former terminus at Port Bannatyne opened. Indeed, despite the closure of the tramway system in 1936, several stretches of the former track bed (minus the rails of course) may still be seen between the Port and Ettrick Bay. If only some enterprising entrepreneur would resurrect even this part of the old system, what a boost for tourism it would be! This view at the Bay terminus shows tram No. 3, one of the popular summer cars with crossbench style seating and canvas blinds which could be lowered appropriately according to weather conditions. The building in the background is the 'American Soda Fountain'. A poster on the front of the tram prominently advertises Clara Kenyon's concerts and dances at the tramway company's Ettrick Bay pavilion, while the painted notice at the rear advises that 'This car runs right across the island to the Sands at Ettrick Bay'. (C. Carter)

Rothesay Tramways car No. 1 on arrival from town at the Ettrick Bay terminus in the mid-1930s. The driver may have been a part-time employee for the summer season, as he has no uniform and is wearing a 'bunnet', whereas the girl conductress, who is reversing the trolley pole in readiness for the return to Rothesay, wears a dustcoat and uniform cap. Car 1 was the first of the ten open crossbench style trams with saloons at either end built on Brill trucks by the Electric Railway & Tramway Carriage Works of Preston. These were delivered in 1902 and used between Rothesay and Port Bannatyne to replace the former horse trams. Once the extension was complete in 1905 they operated through to Ettrick Bay. A further continuation – south along the shore at Ettrick Bay – was planned, but never built; neither were proposed extensions from the Guildford Square terminus in town to Craigmore and also to Kilchattan Bay via Scalpsie. The final Rothesay trams ran in 1936 on what was Scotland's only island passenger tramway. (B. Williams)

In Edwardian times donkey carriages were popular on the Isle of Bute, particularly at Ettrick Bay, as seen here. This one was owned by Jardine of Port Bannatyne who also hired goat carriages for the enjoyment of holidaymakers and their children. For safety reasons potatoes were attached to the goats' horns! The goats were swum across to Inchmarnock Island, off the west coast of Bute, to graze for the winter months. Archibald Robertson, the Rothesay Tramways Co. general manager, is seen to the right in this picture.

Hackney cars line up for business in East Princes Street, Rothesay, near Albert Pier in the early 1920s. Rearmost is SJ 198, a green six-seat Argyll 20 h.p. landaulette of 1919 owned by Charles Pullen, who traded as 'Pullen's Motor and Transport Co.' from Bridge Park Garage, Bridge Street, an address later shared with Dundas Fyfe of Motherwell who operated charabancs on the island for a season or two. Ahead of the Argyll is XS 315, an Arrol Johnston six-seater which was one of several taxis owned by J. & A. Martin, whose cab office was just out of view to the left of this scene. Martin owned both motor and horse-drawn cabs and landaus and progressed to motor charabanc operations (see page 30). Also visible in this view, looking towards Guildford Square, are some of McKirdy & McMillan's open charabancs.

With the houses of Battery Place and Mount Stuart Road visible behind, paddle steamer *Glen Rosa* proudly approaches Rothesay Pier on a fine summer morning in the late 1930s, towards the end of her life. Her skipper and helmsman both stand on the open bridge forward of the single funnel, while her decks are packed with a happy throng of passengers preparing to disembark at Royal Rothesay. This was the second vessel to carry the name *Glen Rosa* and was built in 1893 at J. & G. Thomson's Clydebank yard for the Glasgow & South Western Railway fleet. As with other Clyde steamers, she was impressed for use as a minesweeper by the Admiralty during the First World War, but was subsequently returned for service on the firth and later sailed with the LMS Railway fleet until her withdrawal in 1939, by which time she was the last of the old G&SWR vessels. Today Rothesay is served during the summer season by the restored PS *Waverley* of 1947, the world's last seagoing paddle steamer, on her Firth of Clyde sailings.

Rothesay's Thomson Fountain, where Ardbeg Road leads towards the tramway depot (now bus garage) at Pointhouse, and Marine Place runs to the right along the shore. Tram No. 7 is disappearing towards Port Bannatyne en route for Ettrick Bay, while No. 18 approaches on its way to Rothesay. These were both 'crossbench' type cars, with saloons at each end. No. 7 was built as part of the original order for ten electric cars of 1902 on Brill trucks which replaced the old horse tram system introduced in 1882. No. 18 was new in 1903 and built by Brush of Loughborough. Throughout its lifetime the tramway company was largely dependent on summer visitors for the bulk of its revenue, when extra cars were operated and often crewed by student conductors. The system closed on 30 September 1936 with the final car leaving Rothesay for the Port at 11 p.m., driven by Colin Lamont, although the 'official' last tram had departed at 5 p.m. and was manned by Andrew Kernaghan, who had also driven the first electric car in 1902. According to the lore of former Rothesay tram drivers, Brush-built cars 16 and 20 were firm favourites, both being light to brake and easy to feed current for acceleration. The horse tramway had only operated between Rothesay Pier and Port Bannatyne and on a track gauge of 4', whereas the electric system was built to the narrow gauge of 3' 6".

Seen at the same location as the trams pictured above, YS 2051 (RL 558), operated by Western SMT, passes the Thomson Fountain in 1957 en route from Port Bannatyne to Rothesay. Some services travelled via the Shore Road, seen to the right, although this alternative has not been timetabled for many years, all journeys now using Ardbeg Road and High Road which was the former tramway route. Along with several others of the same type, this bus had an unusual pedigree. It was originally a double deck Leyland Titan TD4 new to Glasgow Corporation in 1935, but was sold in 1948 to be purchased by Western, who had it rebodied as a single decker of Tiger TS7 specification by Burlingham of Blackpool. A number of other vehicles received similar treatment, including some former Sheffield Corporation Leylands.

The Rothesay Tramways Co. started its own bus services in 1925 to combat competition from several small businesses on the island which were adversely affecting revenue. The next stage was to acquire these independent operators and this took place over the years to 1936. In September of that year the last tram ran on what had been a particularly busy service, especially during the summer months when Bute's population could easily double with visitors. One of the opposing busmen taken over by the tramway company was McKellar of Craigmore in 1931, and his charabancs were then painted in the blue livery of the tramway company's buses. Pictured here at Kerrycroy with driver John Black is SL (not SJ) 754, which had started life in the early 1920s in Clackmannanshire. This was a little 12-seat model T Ford which was numbered 19 but only operated until 1934 before being disposed of, as even at that time it was regarded as being ancient in comparison with other members of the tramway company's fleet.

Martin Brothers of Rosehill, Academy Road and later East Princes Street, Rothesay, was one of several small bus and coach proprietors serving the Isle of Bute. The picture shows SJ 527, one of three Morris charabancs purchased in 1926. This one was a 20-seater, usually driven by Bryce Martin who later drove buses for the SMT-controlled Rothesay Tramways Co. after Western SMT acquired the Martin business in 1932. Martin Brothers operated 'Round Bute' tours and also a service between Rothesay and Ettrick Bay in opposition to the electric trams. This Morris was described in licensing records as being painted the colour of claret, and in this view appears to be gaining admiring glances from the youngsters in the foreground.

SJ 787 was a 14-seat Albion LB41 owned by the Kyles of Bute Hydro (or Hydropathic Hotel to give it its full, grand title) at Port Bannatyne. This wee bus led a fairly sheltered life, mainly running from the hotel to connect with steamers at Rothesay Pier where this photograph was taken. Guests, who were generally of the more prosperous sort, were conveyed with their luggage to and from the Hydro. With its smart livery of two shades of green, divided by a cream waistband, this Albion was a long-lived and thus well-known vehicle on the island, since it ran in Rothesay from new in 1934 until eventual withdrawal in 1956, when the hotel decided to relinquish its bus service and gave up its operator's license.

The Rothesay Tramways Company Ltd. was incorporated in 1879 and in 1899 came under the control of the British Electric Traction Co., which also operated the Airdrie & Coatbridge Tramways and the Greenock & Port Glasgow Tramways. BET also had a major interest in McKirdy & McMillan Ltd., operating both horse-drawn and motor vehicles on the Isle of Bute. Rothesay Tramways had to endure competition from various small bus operators on the island including A. & J. Bell of Rothesay with Chevrolets and Albions; C. W. Brennan of Craigmore (Beardmore and Bean); Wm. McGarrity, Rothesay (Morris); Peter McKellar, Craigmore (Ford, Guy); and Martin Bros., Rothesay (Morris, Albion). Most of these owners duplicated the tramways services to Port Bannatyne and Ettrick Bay and also offered tours around Bute. In order to combat the increasing loss of revenue to the busmen, Rothesay Tramways started its own bus service in 1925 with three Albion Viking 18-seat charabancs on the Ettrick Bay route, where Martin's and Bell's were particularly competitive. The tramway company steadily increased its bus fleet and also began to buy out its rivals. By the end of electric tram operations in 1936, all the above-mentioned firms had been acquired, leaving Yeates's Bus Service as the sole remaining operator (and its Canada Hill service provided no competition). Also in 1936, the tramway-associated McKirdy & McMillan bus operations were taken over and bus services on Bute continued under the old Rothesay Tramways title until 1949 when Western SMT absorbed the island operations and repainted all vehicles into its red and cream colours. The photograph shows one of the last vehicles to carry the Rothesay Tramways name, as well as its crimson and grey livery. It was SJ 1049, one of three AEC Regals bodied by Burlingham of Blackpool and delivered in 1946.

Ettrick Bay was naturally described in glowing terms by Rothesay Tramways' advertisements for its tram and bus services from town. One such ad claimed it to be a 'children's paradise, 30 minutes from Rothesay by either electric tramway or by the company's blue buses de luxe'. Facilities at the bay included a tea room and soda fountain, while sand-building, children's sports, amusements, games and aeroplane flights and stunts were also offered. During inclement weather there was 'spacious shelter free to our car passengers' – referring to those who had come by tram or bus. This busy scene looking towards the north end of the bay shows one of a large fleet of former Scottish Transport Tilling–Stevens buses introduced in 1937 as replacements for the withdrawn trams. They dated from 1931, but their original bodies by Brush of Loughborough were replaced before arrival at Rothesay with new open-sided bodywork by Burlingham of Blackpool, which was a reminder of the style of the old trams. Many survived until the late 1940s.

The Rothesay Tramways Co. operated its last tramcar in September 1936 and substituted buses on the former tram route. Having been under the control of Western SMT since 1932, the company instituted a novelty miniature railway of 15" gauge in June 1936 to provide fun rides for the public adjacent to the terminus at Ettrick Bay. The coal-burning steam locomotive, named *Samson*, was an American-built Cagney 4-4-0 which had been originally supplied in 1903 to C. W. Bartholomew of Blakesley Hall, Towcester, Northants, and then passed to John Sword of Ayr, general manager of Western SMT, who purchased it for his son William (who later also became Western's manager). *Samson*'s regular driver Angus MacQueen is seen at the controls in this view from 1938. He later became Western's local manager at the Pointhouse depot, Port Bannatyne. At the top right of this picture the bodies from two former Rothesay trams, which had in previous years made so many journeys from town to this very location, may be seen. The railway was closed and the track removed in 1943, but it then operated at Millport for a couple of seasons at the end of the Second World War. *Samson* is believed to be still in existence at Strumpshaw Hall, Norfolk.

Opposite: Rothesay Pier on a summer afternoon in 1934. The clock on the tower of the turreted pier buildings reveals that the time is 4.30, and the then brand new paddle steamer *Caledonia* is edging outwards into Rothesay Bay from her position between the *Duchess of Argyll* and the *Duchess of Fife*. *Caledonia* is sailing for Craigmore, Largs and Millport, her decks well-laden with homeward-bound holidaymakers and day trippers, while the *Duchess of Argyll* in berth 1 will shortly depart for Wemyss Bay, Dunoon, Gourock and Greenock. The former vessel was no less than the fifth paddle steamer to carry the name *Caledonia* and was launched in 1934 at Denny's Dumbarton yard for service with the Caledonian Steam Packet Co. (which also owned the two *Duchesses* visible). Sailing on the firth until 1969, she was renamed *Old Caledonia* and later bought by brewers Bass Charrington who moored her on the Thames until 1980 when serious fire-damage ended her life. One wonders if the boy on the roof of the pier buildings on the right was a steamer enthusiast of the thirties enjoying a bird's-eye view. The lorries in the foreground were owned by local carriers and contractors Meikle & McKellar (another Bute-based 'M & M' in addition to McKirdy & McMillan). McKellar had been a Clyde steamer purser who left to start a motor delivery service for general goods around Bute brought by cargo boats calling at Rothesay Pier. Cabin trunks and other weighty items of luggage belonging to the wealthier longer-stay holidaymakers were also carried to and from the pier.

From the days of the horse-drawn coaches, the Kingarth Hotel at the southern end of the island was used as a refreshment stop on 'Round Bute' tours. This view shows two new 14-seat Fiat charabancs in the fleet of McKirdy & McMillan in July 1926. These were SJ 524 (behind) and SJ 525, both finished in a striking yellow livery. Driver Hughie MacDonald poses with a foot on the running board beside his mate John 'Dinks' Gillies.

In contrast, fifty years later at the same location, these two 1969 Leyland Leopards belonging to Western SMT typify the coaches in use in the 1970s. OAG 528H, operating the 'Round Bute' tour, and OAG 535H, on a Dunagoil tour, were Alexander-bodied dual-purpose vehicles used both for service and touring work and painted in Western's smart black and white livery of the time.

Double deck operation was introduced to Bute in the late 1930s by Western SMT, a decade before the company absorbed the Rothesay Tramways bus fleet, which although technically under Western control since 1932 had continued to operate using its own name, virtually retaining independence until this arrangement ended in 1949. Seen at Guildford Square in August 1958 about to leave for 'the Port' and Ettrick Bay is CS 4509, still bearing its former Kilmarnock-based fleet number KD 93 before receiving a Rothesay 'R' code. This was a Leyland Titan TD4 dating from 1937, which had entered service with Leyland-built bodywork but was rebodied as seen by Northern Counties in 1949. Passing the departing bus is HUE 829, a big Austin Princess taxi which had been new in 1949 and was one of several in McKirdy & McMillan's private hire fleet. Guy and Leyland double deckers were also used during the summer season on the Canada Hill service by McGill's Rothesay Motor Services, but as a schoolboy visitor 'doon the watter' I was particularly fond of the bus illustrated above since CS 4509 was fitted with a 'golden' (brass) radiator, which made it rather special in the eyes of a young transport enthusiast.

The scenic drive from Rothesay to the splendid viewpoint of Canada Hill was operated by Robert Yeates until 1955 when McGill's Bus Service of Barrhead took over operations under the 'Rothesay Motor Services' title. On an August evening in 1964 Duple- (Midland) bodied Bedford SB, registration RVA 220, climbs towards the summit. This bus had started life in 1958 with Isaac Hutchison of Overtown, serving the industrial area around Larkhall, Motherwell and Wishaw. After sale to Rothesay it ran on Bute, still in its former blue and cream livery, until 1965 when McGill's sold their island outpost to Western SMT, although no buses were involved in the takeover.

Stranger on the shore . . . This former Youngs' Bus Service Daimler of 1944 was an unusual visitor to Bute. Youngs' fleet passed to Western SMT in 1951 and this wartime vehicle with lowbridge 'utility' type bodywork by Brush of Loughborough was then sent to assist the Rothesay allocation during the busy summer season. No attempt was made even to paint out the former owner's name, and it continued to operate in Youngs' colourful orange, maroon and cream colours for a period. XS 5587 (S 36) had been one of four Daimlers delivered to YBS during wartime, and after hostilities ended many more entered their fleet. It is seen at Port Bannatyne, and close inspection of the original photograph interestingly reveals the destination to read 'Port Bannatyne via Tram Line' (despite the fact that the trams had disappeared in 1936), signifying that the bus travelled via Ardbeg Road and High Road, as opposed to via the Shore Road which was used by certain journeys for many years.

Seen at Rothesay pierhead stance for 'Round Bute' tours in August 1958 is one of several Maudslays formerly in the fleet of Youngs' Bus Service, Paisley, which came to operate in Bute with Western SMT. XS 6983 had been new in 1950 to YBS as their No. 200, becoming 2200 with Western on its acquisition the following year. It was one of only two half-cab Maudslays in the fleet, with bodywork by Scottish Aviation of Prestwick Airport, the others all having full-fronted coachwork by Brockhouse of Clydebank.

GE 2160 was a Halley lorry (No. 11 of 1928) with the handsome and distinctive V-shaped radiator fitted to these Scottish-built commercials of the period. The United Co-operative Baking Society had a large fleet of delivery vehicles, many of which were Albions and Halleys, whose factories lay only a short distance apart at Scotstoun and Yoker respectively. During the Edwardian period UCBS had built their own lorries which they named 'Unitas' under license from Morton's Belhaven Engineering Co. of Wishaw. This view, with driver Alex MacKechnie, was taken at the Co-operative-owned Roseland holiday camp on Canada Hill overlooking Rothesay Bay, where the Halley would appear to have been delivering or uplifting the hampers seen to the right. The notice on the tree behind the wall ominously reads 'Warning – campers are warned that this wood is dangerous'.

The UCBS was based in McNeil Street, Glasgow, on the south side of the River Clyde opposite Glasgow Green. On Bute there was a branch bakery in East Princes Street, Rothesay, which is seen in the background of this late 1920s photo. The decorated UCBS delivery van was Morris Commercial No. 3 of 1927 carrying promotional slogans around the roof, including 'Co-operation Unites Producer & Consumer'. The name of the driver is not known, nor that of the shop assistant smiling through the window, which carries adverts for 'Brooklyn cream cakes' and 'malted fruit loaf', both UCBS bakery products.

The only major haulage contractor and carrier in Bute today is MacKirdy of Rothesay. The firm has a long pedigree going back to 1870 when the present John MacKirdy Jnr.'s great grandfather (also John) founded the general haulage and coal merchant's business with a horse and cart in Bishop Street, Rothesay. MacKirdy remained there until the 1980s when their base moved to its present site in Cotton Mill Lane, off the High Street. (Incidentally, there was no connection between John MacKirdy the contractor and Andrew McKirdy the carriage hirer – see page 21.) Two Ford tippers were the first motor lorries in the fleet in the 1920s, followed in 1930 by the first new vehicle. This was a 2-ton, 6-cylinder petrol-engined Commer Centaur supplied via agents Hamilton Bros. of Paisley. Other makes operated over the years have included Albion, Bedford, Leyland, Seddon, Thornycroft and Volvo.

The upper view shows SJ 1586, which was a new Albion Chieftain purchased in 1954 and the first diesel-engined vehicle to join MacKirdy's fleet. Bodywork was by Penman of Dumfries. It is seen loaded with a combine harvester destined for Largizean Farm at the south end of Bute. John MacKirdy stands, pipe in mouth, while Neil Mackay is in the driving seat. SJ 2355 was also an Albion Chieftain, new in 1961, with the later LAD (Leyland/Albion/Dodge) type cab. It is seen loaded with timber and pallets outside the original premises at 34 Bishop Street. Both these lorries were in the grey livery used until the present blue was introduced in the 1960s. Today's fleet consists of four ERF and one Volvo, with an increased emphasis on refrigerated units, although local coal deliveries are still maintained as they were back in 1870.

While McKirdy & McMillan focused on passenger transport operations, the once well-known firm of Meikle & McKellar (see also page 34) concentrated on road haulage and furniture removals. Both companies had started in the days of horse-drawn transport, naturally progressing to motor vehicles on their introduction. In 1909 Archibald Meikle, who had previously been operating a carrier's business, joined forces with Duncan McKellar, a former purser on Williamson's Clyde steamers. With an office on Rothesay Pier, much of M&M's work was handling goods to and from cargo boats and heavy luggage from the passenger fleet. SJ 2041 was a 5-ton Albion Claymore removal lorry new in 1959 with a 1,200 cubic foot Luton style pantechnicon body.

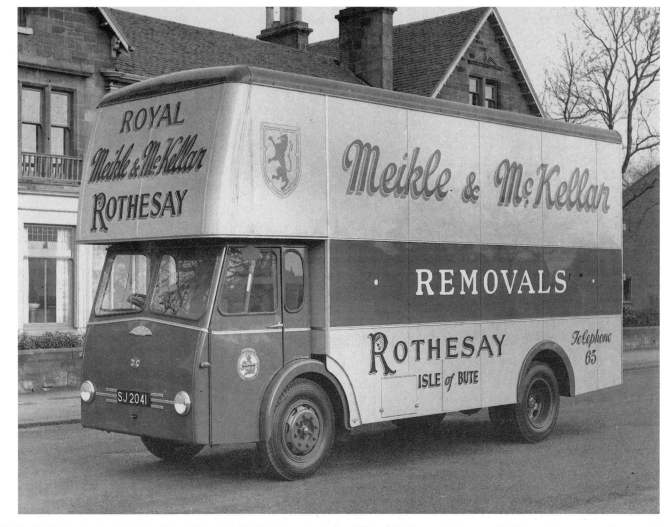

It was finished in McKellar's distinctive red and yellow livery with the accompanying 'Royal Rothesay' slogan, which must have acted as good advertising for the holiday town as this van performed a high percentage of its work on the mainland. In this connection, business for all the island's contractors was greatly assisted from 1950 onwards after the vehicle ferry was introduced between Rhubodach and Colintraive. A further boost to business came in 1954 when car ferries were introduced on the Rothesay–Wemyss Bay sailing. The once-familiar name is no longer seen today as Meikle & McKellar was acquired by Green's Rothesay Carriers in the late 1980s, another firm which has since ceased operation.

A 1954 view of the four-car *Eilean Mor*, a former army tank landing craft and the first of the vehicle ferries (along with the two-car *Eilean Fraoch* [*sic*]) to operate the Kyles of Bute crossing between Rhubodach on Bute and Colintraive on the Cowal Peninsula of Argyll. Later renamed *Eilan Mhor*, she remained in service until 1968. Although there had been a passenger ferry at this point for centuries, the first vehicular ferries were introduced in July 1950 by the Bute Ferry Co., whose chairman and principal shareholder was the Marquess of Bute. The company had taken over operation of the Rhubodach passenger ferry after Colintraive Pier closed in 1948. This scene, from the Bute side, shows YS 5738, an Austin van of 1936 which had to reverse on board since the vessel was bow loading. *Eilan Buidhe*, with capacity for six cars, served the crossing between 1963 and 1969 and was the first to accommodate loading at both ends, allowing drive-through facilities. In 1969 the Bute Ferry Co. was acquired by the Caledonian Steam Packet Co., later absorbed into the Caledonian MacBrayne fleet. An earlier Marquess of Bute had purchased his first locally registered motor car, SJ 123, back in 1912. This was a 40/50 h.p. Rolls Royce shooting brake.

This 20 h.p. grocer's van was an early Ford in Millport. It was purchased in May 1914 by Charles Hunter of 21 Stuart Street, whose family are standing alongside it for this photograph taken in Howard Street. Hunter's family grocery business survived for many years and is still well-remembered by Millport residents. Lettering on the van, which was painted chocolate brown, advertises MacFarlane Lang's bread and also requests customers to try 'Bantam' pure coffee (no grounds!). This must have been one of the very few motor vehicles on Cumbrae at the time and was registered not in Bute but in Renfrewshire, where it received the number HS 699.

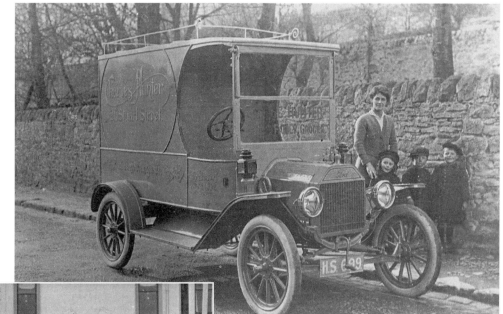

Millport pierhead in September 1965, with the total bus fleet of Morrison's Millport Motors visible. In the foreground are both of the Ford Thames/Martin Walter minibuses purchased by Morrison Bros. for the relatively short-lived service to the caravan site and golf course. As may be seen from the destination board, the fare was sixpence. Parked in the centre of Cardiff Street is DAG 983, in red and cream livery, a 1950 Albion Victor with Scottish Aviation bodywork. This had previously been in the fleet of Paterson, Dalry, and was working the service to and from Keppel Pier via the housing scheme, another route no longer operated. In front of the MacGillivray Arms Hotel is Commer SJ 1315, also with Scottish Aviation bodywork. A bus service to the north end of the island was unnecessary until the commencement in 1972 of the roll-on/roll-off car ferry (see page 47) between Largs and Cumbrae slip.

The first new motor charabanc on the Isle of Cumbrae was a 20 h.p. Ford (SJ 332) which was brightly painted in marine blue and started operations for William Burnie of Stuart Street, Millport, in April 1922. It was similar in appearance to the one owned by Jack Shearer (see page 3) and was one of the few motor vehicles on the island at that period. When Burnie ceased trading, his bus business was continued by John and Donald Morrison who later operated under the name 'Millport Motors', but he retained ownership of his chip shop in Millport. This 1962 view shows Morrison Brothers' garage in Ritchie Street with red and cream liveried CCS 926 of 1949 and SJ 1315 of 1950, two 31-seat Commer coaches both with bodies built by Scottish Aviation of Prestwick Airport. Members of the Morrison family and some of the staff (and Alsatian) stand beside CVS 599, a brand new dark blue Ford Thames minibus with 11-seat Martin Walter 'Utilabus' bodywork. Today these premises are still much the same in appearance, but are now occupied by Horn's garage and service station. Morrison's still operate Millport Motors, however, and now share the bus service between Millport and the Cumbrae slip with Sandy Wright's Cumbrae Coaches, which commenced business in June 1986, taking advantage of the more relaxed licensing which followed government deregulation of bus services. (Walter Kerr)

From 1977 the Isle of Cumbrae became much more accessible to motorists. This ferry of the same name entered service that year on the crossing between Cumbrae slip and Largs (visible in the background). The eighteen-car vessel was so-named as the result of a competition won by Millport schoolchildren and is usually to be found today serving the Caledonian MacBrayne crossing between Portavadie and Tarbert. The scene above at Cumbrae slip dates from 1978 when the Volvo estate car was brand new.

For full details of all books currently available from Stenlake Publishing, and to order copies, please visit www.stenlake.co.uk. (If you would prefer a printed list and order form please phone or write to us.) All orders to UK addresses are **post-free**, and books can be despatched worldwide for a small flat-rate charge.

Stenlake Publishing Ltd.,
54–58 Mill Square, Catrine, Ayrshire, Scotland, KA5 6RD.
phone +44 (0)1290 551122
www.stenlake.co.uk

Bicycles have typified wheels around the Isle of Cumbrae for generations. Families visiting the island still do today what their parents and grandparents did yesterday – make for Millport and hire bikes from Bremner's, Mape's or Morton's. Another tradition is to pedal round to the west side of Cumbrae to enjoy an ice cream at the cafe at Fintray Bay. On a sunny summer day in 1999 lots of people had done exactly that, as may be seen. Passing the parked cycles is the Stagecoach open top double decker which briefly operated 'Round the Island' tours during the summer seasons from 1999 until 2002. This was B81 WUV, a 1984 Leyland Olympian which had started life with Stagecoach (East London) and is now with Stagecoach (Cumberland). Turning back the clock to the early years of last century, Round the Island tours were just as popular, but operated mainly with horse-drawn open landaus by owners such as Jack Shearer or James Bartholomew of Millport or Clark of Keppel.

Inside back cover: The TSS *Duchess of Hamilton* steams across Brodick Bay towards the pier while SHO 801, an Arran Transport AEC Reliance service bus of 1957 with Duple (Midland) bodywork awaits the arrival of passengers from the vessel. The destination will then be changed to Whiting Bay and for a short time the pierhead will be very busy with both pedestrian and vehicle traffic. This scene dates from August 1969, after which the *Hamilton* had only three further seasons in service until her withdrawal after forty years on the Clyde.

Back cover: Evening shadows fall in June 1982 as day trippers join the Caledonian MacBrayne *Isle of Cumbrae* at Cumbrae slip to return to Largs. Constructed at the Ailsa yard, Troon, in 1977, she was the first purpose-built drive-through vessel on the Cumbrae crossing. Leading the vehicles driving from the ferry is YLS 943R, a 1977 Seddon Atkinson owned by former local haulage contractor Alexander Wilkie of Millport. Note the succinct message 'Go and get Trucked' which Sandy displayed on his cab window. Behind it is a Fiat minibus followed by a Ford Escort and a Volkswagen Caravelle caravanette.